Accounting

A Comprehensive Guide to Small Business Accounting, Budgeting, and Bookkeeping

John Cummings

Table of Contents

Introduction 1

Chapter 1: Accounting Versus Bookkeeping 5

Chapter 2: The Balance Sheet 14

Chapter 3: Working Capital and Liquidity 21

Chapter 4: Accounts Payable 26

Chapter 5: The Income Statement 31

Chapter 6: Inventory and COGS 39

Chapter 7: The Cash Flow Statement 45

Chapter 8: Shareholders' Equity 50

Chapter 9: Financial Ratios 58

Chapter 10: Payroll Accounting and Business Analysis 66

Conclusion 76

Introduction

Running a small business requires you to wear many hats. Perhaps the least liked hat of them all is the accounting or financial hat. Many small business owners are great at setting up operations and marketing their business but fail to keep track of the dollars and cents their businesses earn. As a result, they place themselves in a precarious position.

It is hard enough to run a business well. You need to take care of many different things from your customers, to your employees, to your competitiveness. Neglecting your finances or treating them as a hurdle is a surefire way to get into trouble. Even the simplest of topics can confuse an owner. For example, let's take the case of receipts. Which ones should you save and which ones can you discard? Are there special filing requirements? Do you need to digitize all of your receipts? The questions are endless.

When we venture into the space of financial statements, these confusions become even more immense. Many owners are up to speed with bookkeeping but fail to understand that keeping the books and preparing financial statements are two very different things. This is why this book will begin by giving you a thorough understanding of what bookkeeping is and how it differs from accounting. Accounting is also meant to give you a clear picture of where your business stands but it's a bit more intricate than merely recording expenses and income for bookkeeping purposes.

For starters, you need to understand the differences between bookkeeping and accounting. Bookkeeping isn't as intricate as accounting is but it's the foundation on which the latter is built. There are two primary ways of bookkeeping and you'll be learning about them in detail in this book. For practical purposes, only one of these methods needs to be used, and that is what I will focus on the most.

Once we've left the world of bookkeeping behind, it's time to dive into the balance sheet. It is one of the primary accounting statements that is used to determine the financial position of a business. It has three main portions to it and understanding all of them will help you make better business decisions.

Given how dense the balance sheet is, it's impossible to dive into each and every aspect of it. However, you'll be learning some of the most important portions of it, namely the accounts payable liability account, working capital and liquidity, and the shareholders' equity account. These three items, especially working capital and liquidity, are essential for you to understand when reading and preparing financial statements.

Once you've learned about the balance sheet, we'll move forward and dive into the income statement. This is the second of three important financial statements and can also be the most misleading. A lot of the confusion occurs due to the way in which accounting guidelines specify the recognition of income. You'll learn about the pitfalls of leaning on the income statement too much, along with learning about one of its most important line items, the cost of goods sold or COGS.

Lastly, we have the SCF or statement of cash flows. This financial statement is invaluable and aims to compare the differences between actual cash in the bank and income earned. You'll learn how it does this. Learning all about accounting statements is one thing but using them to make decisions is entirely another. The final chapter in this book is going to give you a few handy ways to compute the value of projects and your business based on cash flows or earnings.

These are some of the things you're going to learn all about in this book. I've written this book in such a way so that even the more non-financial of business owners will be able to understand what accounting is all about. Naturally, I've had to make some assumptions about your knowledge. For instance, I've assumed you're a business owner and that you understand what a profit is and how it differs from a loss.

Other financial terms such as working capital and capital expenditures have been defined. In my experience, business owners understand these concepts but don't know the names by which they're referred to. If you understand these concepts and are looking for a handy guide to figure out how they affect your business, you've come to the right place. This book isn't a replacement for an actual accounting professional of course. Its purpose is to introduce you to basic concepts. My aim is to simplify as many of these concepts as possible.

However, there are certain areas where simplification isn't possible. I've minimized such instances as much as I can and have explained ideas and concepts related to them in as much detail as possible. As you read this book, try to take as many notes as you can. Highlight the definitions of concepts that you think are relevant and record all of your questions for further study. This will help you engage with the material here much more effectively.

The chapters in this book deal with different financial topics so as to allow you to quickly refer back to them when you need to verify information. The chapters don't exist by themselves, since every one of them needs information about basic concepts from the previous chapter. However, if you understand the basics, you can refer to them separately. In fact, if you have any particular doubts about certain topics, simply flip to the relevant chapter and read it.

The topic of accounting might be boring to many, but it's one that you should have some knowledge of as a business owner. It affects your bottom line directly after all. You don't need to prepare your own account statements and books, but you do need to understand what's going into them. So, sit back and read the material in this book at your own pace. Let's begin by understanding the differences between accounting and bookkeeping.

Chapter 1: Accounting Versus Bookkeeping

Bookkeeping and accounting are often thought of as being the same thing, but this isn't correct. Sure, they belong to the same branch of your small business, but their functions are entirely different. Your books are the record of your business' financial data. Accounting and bookkeeping deal with the data that gets entered into the books, but the way they use that data is completely different.

The easiest way to describe the difference between these two disciplines is to say that bookkeeping is just a subset of accounting. An analogy might make the difference much clearer to you. Let's say you were constructing a building. You'll need all kinds of plans to make it a good one. You'll need an architect to create designs and make sure all of them meet specifications. You'll then need to hire workers who will turn these designs into reality.

In this analogy, the building is your business, the architect is your accountant and the construction workers are your bookkeepers. Bookkeepers usually work under direct supervision of an accountant. Their primary task is to record financial data in a manner that makes it easy for accountants to conduct a thorough analysis of that data, and then prepare statements in accordance with government regulations.

These days, the lines between bookkeeping and accounting are blurring. You'll find an increasing number of bookkeepers presenting themselves as quasi-accountants. In fact, many small business owners don't hire bookkeepers, preferring to enter financial data themselves and presenting it to their accountant. I must make it clear that accountants aren't financial analysts by default.

Some of them double as analysts, but an accountant's job is to simply present the financial picture of the business they're representing, in as ethical a manner as possible. Accountants are heavily scrutinized, and they prepare the financial statements of a company according to the Generally Accepted Accounting Principles (GAAP) in the United States.

If you're an owner who likes to record their own bookkeeping entries, you'll probably be able to make sense of your business' condition by looking at the entries by themselves. However, if your business grows beyond a certain size and experiences many transactions, you'll need the assistance of financial statements to help you make sense of the state of your business. Mere bookkeeping entries won't give you a clear picture of the financial state of your company.

Preparation

Preparing bookkeeping entries isn't too difficult. The most common form of bookkeeping entry is the double-entry system. The double-entry system is an elegant method that is over 500 years old. It addresses many of the issues with a single-entry system. The single-entry system is the default approach that many business owners take when they first begin their businesses. The single-entry method prioritizes cash coming in and leaving the business. For example, if the business earned $200 in revenue, a line time is added that indicates an increase of $200. If $500 needs to be paid out, a -$500 is entered.

As transactions increase and as their nature becomes more complex, a single-entry system cannot hope to provide accountants with an overview of what the business' accounts look like. This is where the double-entry system shines. The double-entry system is based on a very simple concept. Every transaction affects two accounts. If one account increases in value, another must decrease.

All entries are made in a general ledger which contains two columns, one on the left and one on the right. Bookkeepers and accountants classify all transactions in one of the following categories:

- assets
- liabilities

- equity
- revenue
- expenses
- gains
- losses

The double-entry system is underpinned by a simple accounting equation that is as follows:

Assets = Liabilities + Shareholder's equity

Shareholder's equity is the amount of a business that a shareholder owns. Liabilities refer to the amount of money borrowed, and assets refer to what the business owns (such as property, goods in inventory, cash, and so on.) Assets go on the left-hand side of the ledger and the other two entries go on the right.

Any addition to the left-hand side of the ledger (assets) is called a debit, and an addition to the right-hand side is called a credit. These terms don't adhere to their English definitions so don't confuse the two. Let's look at an example to make sense of this. Let's say you opened your company and recorded your first transaction, which was to invest $20,000 of your own cash to buy $20,000 worth of company stock.

In the general ledger, $20,000 will be added to the company's cash balance since you'll deposit this amount into your business' account. Since cash is an asset, it belongs on the left-hand side of the ledger. Since cash is being added, $20,000 is debited. Note that the cash balance still increases despite us using the word "debit." Remember, we're not using the English definitions of debit and credit here. These words can imply both an increase and decrease of money.

Now that the left-hand side is taken care of, we need to look at the right-hand side. Since the left-hand side received cash of $20,000 (debit) we need to add the same sum of money to an account on the right-hand side (credit.) This ensures both sides of the ledger are balanced. Since you'll receive shares in the company, you'll own $20,000 worth of equity as a shareholder. Therefore, you'll add (credit) $20,000 to the shareholder's equity on the right-hand side of the ledger. Here's what your ledger will look like:

Assets	Liabilities and shareholder's equity
$20,000	$20,000

In equation form here's what it will look like:

Assets = Liabilities + Shareholder's equity → 20,000 = 0 + 20,000

Both sides are in balance. Now let's say your business earns revenues of $200. Revenues increase cash and ultimately increase equity. Therefore, you will debit cash (since it's on the left) and credit equity or a revenue account (since it's on the right.) In both cases you're adding $200, but since one is on the left and one is on the right, we use the word debit and credit respectively. Here's what your ledger entries will look like:

Account Name	Debit	Credit
Cash	20,000	
Equity		20,000
Cash	200	
Service revenues		200

Service revenues will ultimately be added to shareholder's equity. Typically, debit entries are recorded first, and their corresponding credit entries are recorded in the column below them, with the credit entry's name staggered to indicate it balances the previous debit. In larger businesses, you'll often see more than one credit entry offsetting a debit entry.

This is normal. There's no rule that says that credits and debits must have a one to one numerical relationship. All that matters is that their amounts balance each other out. Also note that it isn't necessary for a right-hand side account to offset a left-hand side account.

Let's say your company now purchases a vehicle using cash. The new vehicle is an asset, so it goes on the left-hand side of your ledger. However, you paid using cash which is also an asset on the left-hand side. How will this be represented?

Account Name	Debit	Credit
Cash	20,000	
Equity		20,000
Cash	200	
Service revenues		200
Vehicle	5,000	
Cash		5,000

Since our cash level has decreased by $5,000, it's been credited. Again, we use the word credited because cash goes on the left-hand side of our ledger equation. A decrease on the left-hand side is a credit. A decrease to the right-hand side is a debit. What does our equation look like now?

Assets = Liabilities + Equity → Cash + vehicle = liabilities + equity → 15,200+5,000 = 0+ 20,200

Both sides perfectly balance each other out. Double-entry systems form the basis of accounting statements. The general ledger that we just created for our sample business forms the basis of creating a balance sheet, income statement, cash flow statement, and a statement of stockholder's equity. If you're a small business, the first three will be more than enough to communicate the position of your business to anyone on the outside looking in.

You can see that double-entry bookkeeping doesn't provide an easy way for us to analyze what's going on with a business. We need to visualize what our accounting equation will look like based on the entries in the general ledger. Given that both sides of the equation can result in credits and debits, it can be tough to quickly develop numbers pertaining to the business.

For example, in our latest scenario, let's focus solely on the general ledger (GL). We see that we started out with $20,000 in cash and this increased by $200. However, cash is then credited (decreased) by $5,000. We received an asset in exchange for this cash but the precise effects of the revenue we earned previously on the right-hand side of our equation isn't obvious.

Now, imagine a business that has hundreds of these lines over the course of a month. This is what the average small business deals with. It's impossible to sit down and figure out what a business' financial health looks like using just the GL. What's needed is an accounting statement that helps us figure out what's going on. This is why you can't rely on bookkeeping alone.

These days, accounting software allows you to enter your bookkeeping entries and assign them to various GL accounts. A GL account refers to the entries we made when assigning money in the tables above. Cash, service revenues, and so on are GL accounts. These accounts are linked to entities in accounting statements. Accounting software uses the numbers linked to these accounts to create financial statements.

You can see how crucial bookkeeping is to accounting, and also how it's a subset of the practice. Let's now move on and examine the first accounting statement, the balance sheet.

Chapter 2: The Balance Sheet

The balance sheet is one of the most important financial statements that is connected to your business. It presents a company's financial position at the end of a specified date. It provides everyone a look into what a company owns and what it owes. If you ever apply for financing, your loan officer will first take a look at your balance sheet to figure out where your business stands.

The accounting equation you learned in the previous chapter is directly tied to the way the balance sheet is constructed. It has three portions: Assets, liabilities, and stockholder's equity. The latter two add together to equal assets. Let's examine them one by one.

Assets

Assets are what your company owns. They've been acquired through transactions and are the things that help your company make money. In accounting terms, they have future economic value. Costs that have been paid in advance but haven't expired are also assets. Some examples of these include prepaid insurance, legal fees, rent, and advertising. A company's asset accounts usually include the following:

- cash

- accounts receivable - money that your business has to receive from customers
- inventory
- buildings and land
- goodwill - I'll explain this shortly
- equipment and machinery

Assets go on the left-hand side of our accounting equation and will therefore have debit balances. An increase in their value is a debit while a decrease is a credit. Assets are classified on a balance sheet under the following headings:

- current assets
- investments
- property, plant, and equipment
- intangibles

The amounts that are reported on the balance sheet are actual costs recorded at the time of the transaction. For example, if a company buys land, the value of the land on the balance sheet will remain the same as the years go by, even if the land increases in value. This is called the cost principle in accounting and obliges accountants to report every asset at cost price.

There is another guideline that accountants follow to present an accurate picture of a company's assets. If the value of an asset decreases over time, accountants present the decreased value. For example, if your company makes electronics and you have inventory that was originally valued at $30,000 but went unsold for a year, that inventory may now be worth just $2,000 on the market. Your accountant will report the lower value.

Lastly, accountants have to present values according to expectations. This applies to assets such as accounts receivables (AR). If your customers owe you $10,000 but you expect to collect just $5,000, your accountant will report the lower number. To satisfy double-entry bookkeeping standards, an amount of $5,000 will be credited (added since it will go on the right) to an "allowance for doubtful accounts" account on your ledger.

A quirk that often confuses business owners is depreciation. Assets such as buildings and land are recorded at cost value and are then depreciated over their lifetime. Depreciation is a fancy way of saying that their value will be reduced by a certain percentage over time. If your company owns property, this is particularly confusing. Your balance sheet will show a reducing value for the property but as everyone knows, real estate generally appreciates over time.

This is a loophole in the accounting system that currently exists. GAAP needs to account for a wide variety of assets, and this is why such occasional head-scratching principles appear. Another loophole that exists is with regards to goodwill. Small companies won't carry this line item, but larger companies do. Let's say company A wishes to purchase company B.

If company B's equity (which is calculated by subtracting liabilities from assets) amount to $100,000, this is the accounting definition of what the company is 'worth.' However, from a business perspective, the fair market value could be greater or lesser than this amount. You'll shortly learn why. If company A pays $200,000 for company B, the additional $100,000 paid needs to be accounted for. This is where goodwill comes in. It's a catch-all line item that accounts for the excess money paid as an asset. If company A later determines that they paid too much for B, they'll record an impairment against goodwill that reduces the amount of goodwill on the balance sheet.

Liabilities

Liabilities are what a company owes. Typically, the bulk of a company's liabilities are its debts owed to creditors. Liabilities are also a claim against the company's assets. This is because if liabilities aren't paid, creditors can claim assets as payment in return. Money received for future services are also recorded under liabilities. Typically, companies defer the recognition of such revenues and instead record it as a liability on their balance sheet.

Here are some of the accounts that come under the liabilities section of the balance sheet:

- accounts payable
- interest payable
- income taxes payable
- customer deposits
- bonds payable
- lawsuits payable
- warranties payable

Liability accounts usually go on the right-hand side of the accounting equation and will therefore have credit balances. All liabilities are classified as current or long-term on the balance sheet. As a rule of thumb, those liabilities that are due within a year are considered current. Let's say the company has drawn a loan that requires repayment in monthly installments over the next five years. How is this reported?

Well, the principal that is due over the next 12 months is reported as a current liability. The remaining principal is treated as a long-term liability.

Shareholders' Equity

The shareholders' equity is the last section of the balance sheet. According to the accounting equation you learned in the previous chapter, the sum of the equity and liabilities must equal the assets of the company. In many cases, accountants prepare a statement of assets and liabilities and subtract the liabilities from the assets to report the equity figure.

If your company is a sole proprietorship, the words "owner's equity" will be used in this section. Like assets and liabilities, there are different GL accounts that correspond to this section of the balance sheet. Some examples include:

- common stock
- paid-in capital in excess of par value
- retained earnings
- accumulated other sources of income

Like with liabilities, these accounts will have credit balances. On the balance sheet, the shareholders' equity section is divided into the following sections:

- paid in capital - this is money paid by shareholders in exchange for stock
- retained earnings - this is the amount of net income earned from inception less the dividends paid to shareholders since inception
- accumulated other comprehensive income - income that hasn't been reported as net income on the income statement; examples include foreign currency transactions and pension liabilities
- treasury stock - shares of a company that have been repurchased from stockholders

I must point out that the owner's equity is not equal to the fair market value of the company. This is because the equity on the balance sheet is a function of the assets a company has, and the assets aren't carried at fair market value. Let's look at a simple example. Assume your company has bought a laptop worth $1,200 and has zero liabilities. The equity in your balance sheet will also read $1,200 (since assets = liabilities + equity).

However, the fair market value of your computer might be $500 since it's a used item. Therefore, the fair market value of your company is far less than what the equity number is. Remember that equity and asset values are accounting numbers and don't always reflect fair market value. Revenues, gains, and expenses affect equity with the first two items increasing it and the third decreasing it.

The bookkeeping entries from your GL are directly used to build a balance sheet, and this financial statement is the backbone of your business.

Chapter 3: Working Capital and Liquidity

The balance sheet is important from both a financial and business perspective. It gives a prospective creditor a good understanding of what your business looks like. The way it does this is by providing a clear picture of what your business owns and what it owes. From your own perspective, your balance sheet will also help you figure out what your working capital situation is like.

Working capital is calculated by subtracting current liabilities from current assets. It isn't a line item on any financial statement but is a direct measure of how much cash you have in the bank. This cash is what you'll use to finance operations. If you owe more than what you own, you'll have no cash. For example, let's say you have $50,000 in cash (asset) and owe the bank $60,000 in unpaid principal over the next year. You might have cash in the bank but clearly, that cash is spoken for. You need it to pay the bank.

Therefore, spending it on purchasing more inventory or increasing salaries is unwise. Some of the factors that affect working capital include:

- Your inventory levels and what you can get for it - you might record inventory at maximum market value, but if the market won't pay more than 50 cents on the dollar for it, your working capital is lower than it seems.

- Day sales outstanding, or DSO - this is a measure of how long it takes you to collect payment from your customers. You might recognize revenue this month but if it takes your customers two months to pay their bills, it isn't real cash. Increasing accounts receivables can inflate working capital, but it isn't cash.

- Profitability.

- Amount of money borrowed - you can increase cash by drawing long-term loans or by refinancing current liabilities to longer term payments.

- Equity investment - cash can increase by issuing more stock.

Closely tied to working capital is the liquidity of your company. Liquidity is your company's ability to pay its bills. In the example we just looked at, your company owes an amount greater than its cash on hand. This means it cannot clear its bills and is illiquid. You can make it liquid by selling goods for profits or by raising cash through financing.

Working Capital Versus Liquidity

Many business owners prioritize working capital levels for liquidity or vice versa. It's tough to balance both metrics but doing so is crucial for the health of your business. For example, a small business owner who sells goods for a profit on 60-day credit cycles will have high working capital levels. This is because once they sell their goods, they recognize revenues and add it to their assets under accounts receivable.

This boosts current asset levels and therefore increases working capital. However, it's accounts receivable that has been boosted, not cash. They could theoretically have zero cash and $100,000 in receivables. They can't pay their rent or utility bills using receivables. They need cash to do so. Hence, their working capital is healthy, but their liquidity is bad.

Contrast this with an example of a business that sells products to customers and receives payments instantly. This company needs to pay its suppliers after 60 days of purchase. This credit line is a liability that weighs heavily on the balance sheet. This means their working capital decreases. However, thanks to receiving cash from customers instantly, the company has high levels of liquidity and they can pay their bills. Their assets aren't stuck in inventory or receivables, they're in cash.

You might be wondering, which is better? Truth be told, both are important, however, high liquidity edges out high working capital levels in terms of importance. It's best to have cash on hand whenever possible since this is what pays the bills. Most companies follow the accrual method of accounting. This method recognizes revenue when it is earned (not when cash reaches the account) and expenses when they're incurred (not when they're paid out).

This means cash and revenue recognition can be disconnected from one another. This is why the statement of cash flows exists, so that creditors can figure out the extent of the disconnect. You'll learn more about that later in this book.

Operating Cycle

A company's operating cycle clearly identifies its working capital position and also helps you identify when you can expect cash to hit your company's account. It's the average amount of time it takes for you to invest the company's cash and to receive payment from your customer for the final product. For example, let's say you buy shoes from a wholesaler. This is the beginning of your business journey.

It takes you 120 days to sell all of these shoes to you customers, and your customers pay you instantly. This means it takes you 120 days to invest business assets and to see a return on what you've invested. Your operating cycle is 120 days long.

The length of your operating cycle should be compared to the credit terms you receive. If your supplier extends 30 days credit to you and if it takes you 120 days to recover cash, you need to have cash on hand to pay your suppliers. If your customers pay you after 30 days using credit, your operating cycle extends to (120+30) 150 days. You'll probably need longer credit cycles with your suppliers to account for an operating cycle of this length, or have lots of cash on hand.

The operating cycle is therefore a metric you can use to evaluate your expected liquidity levels. If your suppliers expect to be paid instantly and if your operating cycle is 150 days long, you're setting yourself up to face serious headwinds. The key to improving liquidity is to shorten operating cycles or lengthen credit cycles, preferably both. Here are some of the other items that shorten the operating cycle and increase liquidity as a result:

- reducing the time it takes to collect receivables
- optimizing inventory purchases
- extend credit only to long time customers
- extending credit lines with suppliers
- refinancing current liabilities to longer terms - this increases working capital and places lesser burden on cash, which improves liquidity

Chapter 4: Accounts Payable

Accounts payable is a line item that is recorded under the current liabilities section of a balance sheet. This is a sum of money that must be paid to a creditor, usually a supplier. Note that accounts payable (AP) doesn't include interest owed to the bank. It's reserved strictly for business bills that need to be paid. For this reason, it's classified as a current liability.

The easiest way to think of it is this: your company's AP is your supplying company's receivables. Since this is a liability account, it will have a credit balance. Once the bills are paid, AP is debited (reduced) and cash is credited (reduced). As per the accrual method of accounting, the company receiving goods or services must report the liability on the date (or before) they were received. Expenses are reported as they're incurred, not when they're paid for.

AP processes are usually a bottleneck since companies need to review whether they're paying the right invoice to the right creditors. Typically, they'll review their purchase orders, product delivery reports, invoices, and contracts to make sure the invoiced amount is correct. Due to the nature of double-entry bookkeeping, omitting a vendor's invoice will cause misreporting in two accounts. For example, if you forget to record a repair expense:

- the liabilities will decrease, and this inflates working

capital
- net income increases since the expense isn't recorded

Similarly, recording an expense twice will inflate liabilities and reduce working capital, and will reduce income reported. This means your company's AP process needs to be efficient and up to speed. Companies typically invest a lot of money and time into ensuring payables are processed correctly. These days, you can invest in automated software that makes it easy for you to record and pay your bills on time. It also helps you make the receivables process more efficient.

Purchase Orders and Other Reports

The purchase order (or PO) lists the item that the company wishes to purchase from a vendor. It is sent to the vendor and the AP department at a minimum. More people could receive copies of the PO depending on your company's internal processes. It will indicate a PO number, the date it was prepared, the vendor's name, a contact person, and a description of the items or services being purchased along with the prices and shipping information as pertinent.

Receiving Report

A receiving report is generated once the goods ordered have been received. It might be as simple as a receipt with a stamp indicating that the goods were received on a certain date. Often, the receiving report is prepared in the same format as the PO to enable easy comparison. When the bill comes due, the vendor invoice, the PO, and the receiving report are compared to ensure that all information matches. Some companies refer to this as a three-way match.

Larger companies have a huge number of purchases, and during internal audits, they'll need to preserve all of these documents to enable reconciliation and verification. Even if your company isn't large, it's a good idea to preserve vendor invoices and receiving reports at the very least. It might not make sense to issue a PO for every purchase you make. However, you should maintain this basic audit trail for at least five years or digitize all of your records. This will help you justify the numbers in your financial reports in case the IRS decides to audit you.

IRS Classifications

These days, the gig economy is prevalent, and this means you need to account for whether a person providing you services is a contractor or an employee. The lines can get blurred often. If the individual's services are essential to your business and contribute to the core business for a large period of time, the IRS deems that this individual must be treated as a part-time employee for reporting purposes.

This means once this person issues you an invoice for their services, you'll need to withhold payroll taxes and issue them a Form W-2 instead of a 1099-MISC, which is typically issued to contractors. Make sure you speak to an accountant about the distinctions between a contractor and an employee and identifying them with your accountant.

Internal Controls and Processes

Given the sensitive nature of the payables process, it's essential that you create verifiable and clearly outlined procedures and controls. Not only do these processes have to be monitored, they need to be verified and audited regularly. Companies use vouchers to establish an audit trail. A voucher is literally a document that "vouches for" the legitimacy of a transaction.

Once the three-way verification is complete, a voucher is attached to the relevant documents and is stored. The voucher records all pertinent information about the order as well as the name of the employee who verified the documents. This makes it easy to establish an audit trail. It's a good idea to batch payments to your vendors since this will help you carry out your processes efficiently.

Certain goods and services will be subject to sales taxes. There are two types of sales taxes. The first is the tax on sales taxable goods. The second is a state use tax. One usually applies if the other isn't applicable. Some states may not require you to collect either. The bottom line is that you need to be well-informed and familiar with the laws of your state and collect taxes accordingly.

Payables and the GL

AP is a liability account on the GL, and it has a credit balance. Once a vendor invoice is received, AP is credited and one of the following accounts is debited:

- expense accounts
- prepaid asset accounts
- fixed asset accounts

When a company pays all or part of a recorded vendor invoice, AP is debited, and cash will be credited. As explained before, both of these accounts will reduce in value when this is done.

Chapter 5: The Income Statement

Now that you've learned of the important components of the balance sheet, it's time to move to the second pillar of accounting statements: the income statement. This is one of the most important statements that business owners can use to figure out the health of their businesses. It's also referred to as a profit and loss statement since this is literally what it outlines. It can also be called a statement of income or a statement of earnings.

The income statement shows the profitability of a company during the reporting period mentioned in the statement. Typically, public companies issue financial statements every quarter, with an annual statement summarizing the performance of the preceding four quarters. The primary items that the income statement discloses are revenues, expenses, and gains or losses. It does not list cash receipts or cash paid out.

It clearly lists the profitability of a company and as you can imagine, this is of primary importance. The income statement is structured in the following way:

- revenues and gains
    - revenues from primary operations
    - revenues from secondary operations
    - gains from the sale of assets or from lawsuits

- expenses and losses
    - expenses involved in primary operations
    - expenses involved in secondary operations
    - losses from sale of assets or from lawsuits

The total expenses are then subtracted from the total revenue and this gives us a profit or loss figure. If there's a profit, it's called net income. If it's a loss, it's called a net loss.

Revenues

Revenues from primary activities are also called operating revenues. They refer to money that your business earns by carrying out its regular activities. For example, the primary activity of a retailer is selling apparel or goods. The primary activity of a manufacturer is producing and wholesaling goods. Revenues are not the same as receipts. Remember that under the accrual system of accounting, revenue is recognized when the service is provided and when you have a reasonable expectation that you will collect cash. A receipt is the actual receipt of cash into your bank account.

Let's say you sell your goods with a 30-day line of credit. You'll record revenue once you deliver goods but will record a receipt after 30 days or whenever your customer pays you cash. In some cases, you can have a receipt before revenues. For example, if you require clients to pay you before you provide services, you will have receipts but no revenues. Delivery of services and the probability of collecting cash are crucial to recording revenues.

Revenues from secondary activities are also called non-operating revenues. These are the income you earn from activities that are outside your regular buying and selling of goods and services. Note that you'll often see the words income and revenues used interchangeably. In accounting terms, revenues are the top line of the income statement while income refers to the bottom line, or your earnings. When you refer to these items, make sure you understand the context in which these words are being used.

Revenue can be earned by the sale of long-term assets. For example, let's say you bought a car for your business for $20,000 and depreciated it over the years to a value of $2,000 on your books. You sell this car for $5,000. Technically you've lost $15,000 on this car purchase since you bought it for $20,000 and sold it for $5,000. However, since you're carrying the asset on your books for $2,000 (its book value) you'll record a profit of (5000-2000) $3,000. This income is reported under the gains section of the income statement. Obviously, since your business isn't in the field of selling vehicles, this is a non-operating revenue item.

Expenses

Expenses can be operating and non-operating as well. The ones incurred as a part of regular operations are operating expenses. Expenses are recorded on the income statement during the same period when the revenues are recorded. For example, if you pay your suppliers on a 60-day credit line but recorded the revenue from the sale of an item today, you'll have to record the purchasing expense as well. This is despite paying your suppliers 60 days after you bought the item or its raw materials.

When it comes to expenses, it's very common for companies to record them before paying for them. Just like revenues, expense recording and cash payment will differ. Not all cash outflows from your company account are an expense. For example, you pay a certain amount to your creditors to refinance your loans. Clearly, this isn't an expense since it reduces your current liabilities despite it reducing your cash.

Not every expense is matched to a revenue stream or sale either. For example, salaries, utility payments, and so on are not linked to a sale. Depreciation is also not linked to a sale but is instead linked to an asset. Depreciation is a confusing expense that throws off a lot of people. It's confusing because it doesn't reduce your cash, but it reduces your net income.

Typically, companies need to write down the value of an asset on their books over a number of years. GAAP specifies broad guidelines for accountants to estimate the useful life of an asset. Typically, buildings and real estate are estimated to have a useful life of 30 years. Vehicles have an estimated life of 10 years, as does furniture and other office equipment. Electronics have shorter lives. Accountants reduce the value of an asset proportionately over its useful life. It is possible to reduce the useful life estimate of an asset and depreciate it faster. This will reduce your net income since the depreciation expense will be greater.

Just as how you can make gains from the sale of assets, you can earn losses as well. Like gains, losses are calculated by subtracting the book value from the sale value. From our previous example of a car, if you had sold the vehicle for less than $2,000, you've earned a loss. Remember the point I made earlier about goodwill when talking about the balance sheet a few chapters back?

Goodwill can fluctuate depending on what the company thinks its assets are worth. Companies typically test the value of their acquired assets yearly. If these assets are found to be worth less than what the company estimates it's worth, an impairment is recorded. This is a non-cash expense that reduces net income. For example, let's say company A buys company B for $500,000.

If the total stock of company B was worth $250,000, company A has overpaid by $250,000 for B. This isn't a bad thing by itself. Remember that asset values are not a proxy for market value, and neither is shareholders' equity as a result. It could be that company B has assets that don't deserve to be depreciated, or that it has an earnings stream that is undervalued.

Therefore, on A's balance sheet the $500,000 that B is worth will be split into two parts. The book value of B's assets will be distributed to their relevant line items in A's balance sheet. This amounts to $250,000 as we just read. The remaining $250,000 will be classified as goodwill. The following year, A will need to determine the value of B on its books. If B is still a valuable component of A's business, goodwill is left untouched. However, if B was a bad purchase, an impairment is recorded. If A's accountants determine that B is now worth just $200,000, they'll take an impairment charge of $300,000 which will be recorded as an expense.

Note that this doesn't affect cash. Like depreciation, it's a non-cash expense.

Points to Note

Like asset values, expenses don't always indicate economic reality. This is especially true of older assets and their depreciation expense. For example, if a company has a 40-year-old plant, this asset has outlived its useful life. Therefore, its depreciation expense is zero. However, the company still needs to maintain it and service it to ensure everything runs smoothly. Compare this to a company that has just bought a new facility.

This facility will cost a lot more due to inflation and its depreciation expense will be much higher. This means the second company's net income will be lower than the first's, assuming everything else is equal. Is the second company automatically worse than the first? Well, in this case examining net income doesn't tell us anything. The second company might secure a competitive advantage by moving to a newer plant. Expenses by themselves do not tell us the full story. The business reality of expenses is very different from their accounting picture.

Accountants use estimates to figure out how much an item should cost. They also need to estimate how much of a provision they need to set aside for bad debts and how much they need to charge for depreciation. Confusingly, the rate at which a company depreciates its assets can change to accelerate its value to zero or to reduce its impact on the bottom line. Accountants typically don't do this, but companies can boost net income in lean years by changing depreciation timelines. This is a big reason why the cash flow statement is so important.

Discontinued Operations and Formats

Discontinued operations refer to parts of a company's business that are no longer active and have been dismantled. If a division of a company is sold, this is a discontinued operation. The actual method of reporting discontinued operations is intricate and requires you to study for an accounting degree. As a result, I'm not going to delve into those details. However, note that discontinued operations' income is reported on the income statement just above the net income line.

Income statements come in two formats depending on the complexity of the business. They can be single-step or multiple steps. A single-step income statement uses just one subtraction to arrive at the net income. For example, if a company's revenue and expense streams are easy to understand, both groups are added up and expenses are subtracted from revenues to arrive at net income (earnings.)

If a company has significant expenses from non-operating avenues, a multiple step statement is needed. In this method, sales are first listed, and the cost of goods sold (COGS) is subtracted. Next, operating expenses are subtracted to arrive at the operating income. The net effect of non-operating income is then accounted for. Non-operating revenues and expenses are listed, and the latter is subtracted from the former. This number is then added or subtracted from operating revenues to arrive at net income.

Chapter 6: Inventory and COGS

Inventory is the stuff you buy from your suppliers to sell to your customers. Inventory is reported as a current asset on your balance sheet, and it is a significant asset. It isn't just goods that need to be sold to customers that is inventory. For example, if you're manufacturing a product that has three stages, the value of products throughout each stage is listed as inventory. Note that the dollar value of inventory is listed in your balance sheet, not the number of units. Also, inventory is listed on the balance sheet at cost, not at the price that can be obtained by selling it.

This brings us to the cost of goods sold (COGS). COGS is the cost of the material that you're selling to your customers. Note that the cost of turning raw material into finished product is also included within COGS. For example, if you buy a piece of leather and intend on turning it into a shoe, you need to include the cost of the leather, the cost of additional materials you'll need to finish the shoe, and any other miscellaneous expenses you'll encounter when manufacturing it. Labor costs and factory costs are not included within COGS.

Accounting for Sales

The prices of raw materials and goods your business buys throughout the year will fluctuate. So how should inventory and COGS prices be accounted for? Since prices vary, the margins you'll earn from each sale will also vary. Should you always assume you sold goods for maximum profit or should you assume that you sold them at the highest price? Let's look at an example.

Let's continue our previous one and say you're in the business of buying leather and turning it into shoes. The price of leather varies throughout the year and here's what your purchases look like:

- purchase #1 - $500
- purchase #2 - $300
- purchase #3 - $800

You won't vary your selling prices too much throughout the year since you wish to maintain customer loyalty. Besides, each purchase of leather results in 10 shoes and you keep buying on a continuous basis. It's impossible to tell which piece of leather went into which shoe. Therefore, with your sale price fixed, the profit you earn on each shoe varies. The shoes made from the third purchase will have the lowest profit, those from the second the highest profit, and those from the first somewhere in between. What if a shoe was made with half of its leather sourced from the second purchase and the other half from the third purchase?

It's impossible to account for such variations. There are also implications for your inventory value. How much is your inventory worth given these fluctuating costs? GAAP proposes three ways of accounting for inventory. These are:

- FIFO - first in first out
- LIFO - last in first out
- average - average prices of inventory

These accounting methods prescribe which costs will be accounted for first under COGS. For example, if you use FIFO, you'll earmark your COGS as $500 until those units run out. Next, you'll account for COGS as $300 and then finally $800. If you choose LIFO, the order will be the opposite, and will be $800, $300, and $500.

Under the average system, you'll use the average price of your inventory at all times. In this case it is $533.30. Note that you can change your inventory accounting method after your fiscal year ends. Companies often switch from one method to the other to produce a greater impact on their asset values and net income. This is because inventory and COGS play an important role in determining these numbers.

Periodic Versus Perpetual

Each of these systems can be either periodic or perpetual. Under the periodic system, inventory is updated once, typically at the end of the fiscal year. Purchases of inventory are recorded in purchase accounts and at the end of the year, the amount of inventory in these accounts is added to what's on hand. Due to the way the periodic system works, there is no COGS account to be updated when a sale occurs. When viewing the GL, there is no way to determine the COGS or the inventory on hand.

Under the perpetual system, inventory amounts are constantly updated. There is a COGS account that is debited every time products are sold. Under this system, there will be two journal entries. One records the sale and its effect on cash or receivables, and the other reduces inventory and increases COGS.

This means there are six inventory and COGS accounting systems you can choose from. Businesses aren't limited to these six when accounting for COGS, though. There is an additional method called the specific identification method. If merchandise carries specific identification that allows a business to determine its exact costs, they can increase COGS by the cost of that specific item. For example, if a dealer sells a specifically marked gold nugget that carries its own identification, they can increase COGS by the cost of that nugget.

During periods of increasing costs, LIFO (periodic or not) results in lower profits. This isn't a bad thing, since it will result in lower taxes paid to the government. Companies need to evaluate whether the expense of tracking costs is lesser than the tax benefit adopting LIFO can provide. If the expense is greater, there's no point adopting it. The IRS allows companies to adopt what it calls a dollar value LIFO system. This is an advanced accounting concept that is beyond the capacity of this book. Essentially, it allows companies to adopt LIFO without having to resort to tracking.

Tracking inventory can be complex, and instead of physically counting units on hand, many companies estimate the number of units they have. Needless to say, you need to have robust tracking policies in place to ensure your counts are correct. Overestimating inventory can have massive negative implications for your business.

There are two ways of estimating inventory. The first is the gross profit method. This method uses the gross profit of a product to estimate how much of it is left on hand. Ending inventory is estimated using the formula below:

Ending inventory = Cost of goods available - COGS

Cost of goods available = Beginning inventory + net purchases

COGS = Sales - Gross profit and Gross profit = Gross margin * Sales

Our final formula for ending inventory looks like:

Ending inventory = (Beginning inventory + net purchases) - (Sales - (gross margin * sales))

The second method of estimating inventory is the retail method. This is useful when you have both the costs and the retail prices readily available per unit. Costs and retail are listed in separate columns and the retail and cost values of beginning inventory and purchases are listed for each. The rest of the calculation proceeds according to the table below. I've added example numbers:

	Cost	Retail
Beginning inventory	10,000	14,000
Net purchases	68,000	84,000
Goods available	79,000	99,000
Less: sales at retail		- 90,000
Ending inventory at retail		9,000
Ending inventory at cost	7,110	

The ending inventory number is calculated by multiplying the ending inventory at retail by the cost ratio. The cost ratio is calculated by dividing the amount of the goods available at cost by the goods available at retail. In this case, this works out to (79000/99000) 79%. The ending inventory at cost is (9000*.79) $7,110.

Chapter 7: The Cash Flow Statement

The cash flow statement is officially called "The Statement of Cash Flows." I'll refer to it as the SCF for short. It's one of the main financial statements and it reports the cash used and generated by the company during a specified period. This is usually the same period as is listed on the balance sheet and on the income statement. It lists important cash flows in the following categories:

- operating activities - cash flow from primary business
- investing activities - purchases of long-term investments and upgrades to property, plant, and equipment
- financing activities - capital raising through stock and bonds or debt; repayments and refinancing cash flow are also listed here
- supplemental items - everything else that can't be classified

The SCF is extremely important since it reflects the actual cash flow of the company. The income statement is constructed using the accrual method of accounting and this creates a disconnect between cash in the bank and income recorded. For example, a company can recognize an accrue income at record levels. However, if it can't collect cash on time and collects just pennies on its receivables, the picture isn't as rosy as it looks.

A handy way to measure the disconnect is to compare the cash generated from operating activities to the net income. High quality companies generate more cash than net income. How can they do this? Remember that net income decreases due to non-cash expenses such as depreciation. This amount is added back to net income when preparing the SCF.

Changes to Cash

Understanding the impact that changes to assets and liabilities have on cash can be difficult. Often, the effect on cash that a change to balance sheet items has isn't intuitive. Here's a summary of how cash is affected:

- when an asset increases, cash decreases (except balance sheet cash)
- when an asset decreases, cash increases (except balance sheet cash)
- when a liability increases, cash increases
- when a liability decreases, cash decreases
- when equity increases, cash increases
- when equity decreases, cash decreases

Let's look at these relationships through a few examples. Let's say a company allows its customers to pay in 30 days after selling goods. What happens to cash in this scenario? In this situation, there is zero effect on cash even though income increases. The receivables increase on the balance sheet thanks to revenue being recognized, and the sales account increases. However, there is no cash being transacted so cash is unchanged.

What if a company pays off its payables in full? In this situation, cash will decrease. Therefore, as a liability decreases, cash decreases since cash is used to pay down the liability. If the amount of land a company owns increases, cash will decrease. This is because cash is presumably used to buy the land.

Cash Flow from Operating Activities

The cash generated from operating activities is calculated by converting the changes in accrual records of the current assets and liabilities. This means the following accounts are monitored for changes:

- Accounts Receivable
- Inventory
- Supplies
- Prepaid Insurance
- Other Current Assets
- Accounts Payable
- Wages Payable
- Payroll Taxes Payable
- Interest Payable
- Income Taxes Payable
- Unearned Revenues

- Other Current Liabilities

Non-cash expenses such as deportation and amortization expenses are added back. Changes to current liabilities will be used to figure out cash generated from financing activities, not operations.

Cash Flow from Investing Activities

The cash generated from investment is calculated by evaluating changes to the long-term asset accounts. This means changes in land, buildings, equipment, fixtures, and vehicles are monitored. A critical expense that is listed here is capital expenditures. Usually, expenses are listed in the income statement, but capital expenses are not. From an accounting standpoint, a capital expense is used to create an asset and is therefore not something that decreases net income.

For example, the purchase of new vehicles or property is not an expense that is deducted from revenues. The purchase of assets is not directly connected to the expenses that were undertaken to produce revenues. For example, companies need to pay rent and utility bills to keep the lights on in their offices. This is an operating expense and the cash paid is deducted from revenues on the income statement.

Capital expenses are not subtracted and are instead listed on the SCF. As a company owner, you will have discretion when it comes to designating expenses as operating or capital ones. Don't mistake this for complete freedom though. Reduce your operating expenses too much and you'll end up increasing net income and you'll pay more taxes. Reduce capital expenses too much and move them to operating expenses and you'll reduce your net income and lower your taxes. However, you need to maintain records that justify this classification. Your accountant will guide you as to which expense goes where.

Cash Flow from Financing Activities

Changes to long-term liability accounts create cash flow from investing activities. Changes to stockholders' equity also creates cash flow from financing. For example, if your company's outstanding stock decreases, you've presumably been buying back shares. This is done using cash and will reduce your cash on hand. If you borrow more money from the bank, your cash on hand increases, as does your long-term liability. If you pay yourself or your shareholders dividends, this reduces the retained earnings on the balance sheet and reduces cash on hand.

Chapter 8: Shareholders' Equity

Accounting is often reduced to the accounting formula or equation that I talked about in the first chapter. This is the formula that states that assets equal the sum of liabilities and shareholders' equity. Equity is one of the three primary components, and it's listed in the balance sheet. However, it's an extremely important component of a company's overall health. Public companies routinely publish a statement that tracks the changes in shareholders' equity. You might not need to do this but it's worthwhile examining what equity really means in greater depth.

To understand equity, we first need to look at how legal structures are set up in the United States.

Corporations

Most businesses are set up as corporations and this has several advantages over doing business as a sole proprietorship. For starters, a corporation is a separate legal entity and limits the liability business owners face. If someone sues your company for making faulty products or causing them harm, your personal assets are not exposed to the lawsuit.

Corporations also make it easy for everyone to figure out their ownership structures. Ownership stakes are bought and sold using shares of stock. Companies can raise money by selling pieces of themselves to investors using their shares. These shares can be further bought and sold between buyers and sellers. In these secondary transactions, the company's financial position isn't affected since they aren't a party in the transaction. Issuing shares makes it easy for companies to raise money and compensate investors equitably.

The flip side of corporations is that they're tough to maintain and run. Governing a corporation is a serious task and procedures need to be followed according to the company's bylaws. Another disadvantage is that income derived from corporations is taxed twice. First, the corporation pays taxes on its earnings. If it passes on these earnings to shareholders, this income is taxed at the personal level once again. Company owners routinely search for loopholes to reduce taxes, but eliminating them isn't possible.

Common Stock

If your corporation has issued just one type of stock, it's usually referred to as common stock. Common stockholders elect the board of directors and vote on various company issues. Company owners typically issue different classes of stock to maintain control of their company, despite carving out bigger pieces of it for investors. Each share has voting rights attached to it and different share classes have different voting rights.

For example, a company's A class stock might contain one vote per share, but the B class stock might need five shares to equal the right to one vote. When a business first applies for incorporation with a state, the application will specify the number of shares, classes of stock, and who owns these shares. These shares are called authorized shares. When authorized shares are sold to investors, they become issued shares.

The par value of a share multiplied by the number of outstanding (authorized) shares gives us the legal capital value of the organization. The par value is usually a very small amount that is defined by state law. Remember that equity and business value are two different things. This means the par value of a stock has no bearing on how much a business is worth. Whenever a share of stock is issued, the par value of that stock is recorded in the stockholders' equity account in the GL.

All proceeds that exceed the par value upon sale are credited to a separate stockholders' equity account. All shares that have been issued that haven't been bought back by the company are said to be outstanding. For example, if a company is formed with 100,000 shares and then sells 1,000 of them and buys back 100, it will have 100,000 authorized shares, 1,000 issued shares, and 900 outstanding shares.

The stockholders' equity section of the balance sheet has four components to it. These are:

- paid-in capital

- retained earnings
- treasury stock
- accumulated other comprehensive income

Paid-in Capital

Capital that was received when a company issued stock is called paid-in capital. Some states require corporations to record and separately report the par amount of the issued shares, and also the amount received that was greater than the par amount. The amount received minus the par value is then credited to paid-in capital in excess of par value.

Retained Earnings

As corporations earn net income, they have two choices when it comes to deciding what to do with it. They can pay it back to stockholders as dividends or then can reinvest it into the business. The amount of money that is kept within the company for future reinvestment is retained earnings. In the GL, this account has a credit balance.

Mathematically speaking, the retained earnings of a corporation are the cumulative net income earned minus the amount of dividends paid. The longer a corporation has been in business successfully, the larger its retained earnings will be. A corporation that has incurred a large number of losses in excess of dividends paid will have a deficit or accumulated deficit in place of retained earnings on its balance sheet.

A large retained earnings balance doesn't always mean a large cash balance. This happens because those retained earnings might have been reinvested as capital expenses. To ascertain the true picture of a company's cash levels, you'll need to look at the cash account under the current assets on the balance sheet.

Treasury Stock

Corporations can buy their outstanding stock back from shareholders when they have a lot of excess cash on their balance sheet. Typically, this happens if the managers of the company feel the price of the stock is too low. Buying back stock also boosts the net income earned per share. It boosts the percentage of profits that shareholders will earn for every share of stock. Think of it as the size of the pie remaining the same but the number of claims to the pie decreasing.

Corporation can retire stock they buy back. If they choose to not retire the stock, this stock is called treasury stock. It is the difference between the number of shares issued and the number of shares outstanding. Treasury stock amounts are recorded as a debit balance in the GL. There are two ways of recording treasury stock. The first is the cost method.

Under this method the cost of the stock is debited to the treasury stock account on the GL and cash is credited (decreased, since it belongs on the left-hand side of the accounting equation). If treasury stock is sold, cash is debited. Note that sale of stock in excess of par value is not an income gain. It does not go into the income statement, but lives in the stockholders' equity account instead.

The second is the par value method where the gains from stock sales are calculated by subtracting the sale price from the par value of the stock. Like in the previous method, the gains or losses don't go on the income statement, but are housed under the stockholders' equity account.

Stock Splits

As a company's revenues grow, its stock price typically rises. At some point, the price of the stock becomes too high for it to be traded freely. For example, if a company's shares are trading for $5,000, it's going to attract far fewer potential investors than if it was trading for $50. Secondary market activity isn't of monetary importance to a company, but management typically tries to keep its shares as liquid as possible. This makes it easy to issue new shares and raise more capital.

Splitting a stock is a great way to increase its liquidity. If management decides to split the existing stock on a two for one basis, this will double the number of outstanding shares and will halve the price of each share. The total value of the outstanding shares will therefore remain the same, but the price decreases enabling easier trading.

Small businesses don't need to split their shares, but it's a good thing to know about. As far as the GL and other financial statements are concerned, splitting the stock provides no monetary benefits. The number of outstanding shares increases in line with the split, but that's it.

Stock Dividends

Dividends are usually paid in the form of cash, but a company can pay them using its own stock. These distributions are often referred to as bonus shares. For example, if an existing shareholder owns two shares, they might receive one bonus share as a dividend. This is a one for two stock dividend. A stock dividend that results in less than 25% of outstanding shares to be issued is considered small. Anything above this is considered large.

From the balance sheet's perspective, the value of the bonus shares issued is recorded in the paid-in capital section of the shareholders' equity section. A corresponding entry reduces the balance of the retained earnings on the balance sheet by the same amount.

If a dividend is paid in cash, the amount paid is subtracted from the retained earnings on the balance sheet. The cash on hand also decreases on the balance sheet, and in the SCF the dividend is recorded under the financing activities section.

Chapter 9: Financial Ratios

Not every business owner is an accounting expert. So how do they keep pace with the financial health of their business? Financial ratios that are derived from the accounting statements do the job for such owners. Keep in mind that the ratios are only as good as the numbers they're being fed. If your business misclassifies expenses and gets creative with its accounting, ratios won't help you unearth the true state of the business.

According to GAAP guidelines, accountants must note the basis on which they've prepared the financial statements. The considerations and assumptions they've made when preparing these statements are listed in the notes accompanying the financial statements. If you're ever in a position to analyze another company's books, take special care to read the notes accompanying their statements.

Balance Sheet Ratios

The balance sheet has a number of useful ratios that will help you keep tabs on the financial health of your business. There is no end to the number of ratios you can construct using the balance sheet, so I'm going to highlight the five most important ratios you should keep an eye on.

Working Capital Amount

Technically speaking this isn't a ratio. You've already learned all about working capital and how it ties in with liquidity. Working capital is calculated by deducting the current liabilities from the current assets. The greater your working capital is, the healthier your business is. The amount of working capital you'll need depends on the industry your company is operating in. You can read the chapter on working capital and liquidity in this book to gain more insight into how working capital functions.

Current Ratio

The current ratio is determined by dividing the current assets by the current liabilities. This is also called the working capital ratio. The larger this ratio is, the more secure a business' financial position is. For example, if a company has $100,000 in current assets and $50,000 in current liabilities, the current ratio is two.

Logically, this means that the company has twice the assets needed to pay its immediate bills. However, the current ratio can be misleading. Current assets include cash, receivables, inventory, and prepaid expenses. Current liabilities are debt payments that are maturing within a year. It also includes operating expenses. All of these bills are paid in cash.

If the company has a low cash amount and large receivables and inventory, its position isn't all that secure. For example, if this company were selling shoes, it can't pay its rent using shoes. It needs cash. To avoid such problems, it's worthwhile to discount receivables and inventory when calculating the current ratio.

The discount you'll apply depends on the industry you're in. Sticking with the footwear industry, old stock usually is discounted to 50 cents on the dollar and receivables are typically collected on time. In this case, reducing the inventory by 50% and leaving receivables as is when calculating the current ratio would give us a better picture. In other industries, it might be common for customers to pay 70 cents on the dollar when paying bills. Economic crises might prompt customers to ask for discounts and businesses might collect 50-60 cents on the dollar rather than collect nothing.

Quick Ratio

Another way of avoiding the inventory and receivables problem is to calculate the quick ratio. This is done by dividing cash and cash equivalents by current liabilities. If there's a huge drop-off between the traditionally calculated current ratio and the quick ratio, this means there are a large number of assets held in non-cash form. Some prefer to include receivables when calculating the quick ratio, but this shouldn't be a default approach.

The decision to include receivables depends on the industry. For example, you could include it if the company makes shoes. If it's engaged in providing lengthy credit lines for its customers, more than 90 days or so, then it's doubtful the company can collect 100% of its receivables.

Debt to Equity

Debt in accounting terms means the sum of all liabilities. To calculate it, you'll add current liabilities to long-term liabilities. The debt to equity ratio is determined by dividing debt by the total amount of stockholders' equity. This ratio is sometimes referred to as the leverage ratio. A high number indicates that a company is fueling growth by borrowing money. A low number means it doesn't have too much debt on its books and is paying its bills using retained earnings, including those tied to expansion.

A low debt to equity ratio is preferable but it isn't always a good thing. This is because the tax code in the United States provides benefits to companies that assume debt. Interest paid on debt can be deducted from net income to reduce taxes. Often, companies can generate high rates of return on investment that is well in excess of the interest they have to pay. For example, if a company can borrow money at 2% and it produces growth of 10%, this is a great deal for shareholders.

Companies that have low debt might be relying on issuing stock to fuel growth. This is against the interests of existing shareholders. Think of the company as pie. If the pie keeps growing (earnings growth) and if the number of slices (shares) remains the same, the slices will get bigger. However, if the company creates more slices as the pie grows, everyone ends up pretty much where they started despite the pie growing larger.

Debt to Total Assets

This is also called the assets to liability ratio. Some people also refer to this as the leverage ratio. In certain businesses, it provides a good picture of the leverage of a business, but not always. It's calculated by dividing the total liabilities by the total assets. The higher the number is, the more leveraged a firm is.

Income Statement Ratios

The income statement has three ratios that are pertinent when it comes to analysis.

Gross Margin

The gross margin is one of the most important ratios that businesses must monitor. It's calculated by dividing revenues by COGS. Revenues must be net of any sales, returns, and discounts offered to customers.

Net Margin

The net margin is calculated by dividing the net income by revenues. Net income takes operating costs and interest costs into account, unlike gross margin.

Interest Coverage

This is also referred to as times interest earned, in some quarters. It measures how well the company's earnings cover interest expenses. To calculate it, divide the net income before interest expense by interest expense. This means you'll take all costs into account except interest and taxes. The higher this number is, the better is the company's ability to service its debt. This is especially relevant for highly leveraged companies.

Other Ratios

There are other ratios that combine elements of the balance sheet and income statement. A few others utilize numbers on the SCF as well.

Return on Equity

Return on equity is the true measure of how much of a return an organization is providing its shareholders. Equity is the piece of the company that shareholders own, and it's important to measure how well earnings are stacking up against it. It's determined by dividing the net income by the stockholders' equity.

Free Cash Flow

The SCF doesn't lend itself to too many ratios despite it being an important statement. This is because it allows you to view important information easily. Free cash flow is an important metric and is calculated by deducting capital expenditures from cash provided by operating activities. Some owners choose to divide free cash flow by shareholders' equity to get a clearer picture of the return on equity. Comparing this ratio with the traditional return on equity can uncover potential gaps in evaluating net income.

Limits of Financial Ratios

Remember that ratios are only as good as the numbers that go into them. While ratios provide a nice way for you to look at a company quickly, they don't uncover the inner workings of the company. To do this you'll need to dive deep into the company's statements. For example, net income can be manipulated by misclassifying operating expenses to capital expenses. An even more prevalent accounting gimmick is to change the way in which revenue is recognized. Inventory accounting methods could be switched to boost profits.

Ratios will never uncover such deep issues. Also, resist the temptation to think of certain numerical values as being good or bad. Classifying a ratio value as being good or bad depends on the industry the company is in. In some industries a quick ratio of 1.5 might be great, whereas in others it might be abysmal. Always compare a company to its peers to get a better picture of its performance.

Chapter 10: Payroll Accounting and Business Analysis

If your company has employees, it has to account for payroll and benefits. Payroll accounting applies to a company's employees. However, differentiating between employees and non-employees can be complicated. Generally speaking, if you can control which tasks will be performed by a person and can control how those tasks will be done, the person performing the task is an employee.

Your duties with regards to employees are as follows:

- you will need an employer identification number or EIN from the IRS
- you will have your employees fill out the Form I9 for everyone hired in the US
- have them fill out Form W4
- record their hours worked and money earned
- withhold social security, medicare, income taxes, and other deductions
- remit these withholdings to the IRS
- issue paychecks to employees
- provide them with the W2 form by January 31
- file forms W3, 941, and 940, detailing the various aspects of employee contributions and payments you made throughout the year

These days, many companies hire independent contractors to complete tasks. These people are provided a 1099-MISC that indicates the amount of money they were paid. Payroll accounting is a complex subject, primarily because it involves a deep understanding of the way the IRS requires employers to withhold and remit benefits.

From a purely accounting perspective, recording payroll isn't too complicated. Salaries and wages paid are an expense item that reduce cash and are recorded as such in the GL. Covering the taxation aspect is beyond the scope of this book. You'll be best served by referring to the IRS's website at www.irs.gov or reading a book that covers the specifics of small business taxation.

Conducting Financial Analysis

Businesses often need to decide the ways in which they'll spend their money. They'll have to choose between investing in one asset or another. The easiest way to decide between competing choices is to pick the one that provides the highest return on investment, or ROI. However, determining ROI isn't always easy. This is because you'll have to calculate returns over a long period into the future and it's tough to relate future value of cash flows back to the present. For example, is it better for you to choose $100 today or $105 five years in the future?

Money has what's called time value. A dollar today is not worth a dollar a year from now. Inflation ensures that this will be the case. However, there's also the problem of opportunity cost to consider. If a business has two projects that they could potentially pursue, but have to pick just one of them, which one should they pick? If one provides an eight percent rate of return and the other provides five percent, the smart choice is to go with the one that provides the greater rate of return. If hanging onto the cash and letting it grow in savings offers a better choice, then this is the path a company should take.

Central to the subject of the time value of money, is the net present value or NPV. The NPV is calculated by 'discounting' future cash flows to the present and adding their values together. Discounting is a process where the rate at which money can potentially grow in that time is taken into account. For example, if you let money sit in an investment that returns 8%, any other potential investment choice needs to clear that hurdle rate.

Eight percent becomes the value at which your money grows at a minimum. The potential investment's future cash flows are discounted back to the present at this rate and if their sum is compared to the primary choice. Whichever is greater offers the better potential investment. Strictly speaking, NPV is not an accounting subject and to learn more about this I highly recommend reading *The Theory of Investment Value* by John Burr Williams.

There are four ways in which businesses can use their financial statements to make investment decisions. These are:

- accounting rate of return
- payback
- NPV
- IRR

Let's look at them in turn.

Accounting Rate of Return

This method of evaluating an investment is called a non-cash, non-discounted model. You'll shortly understand why it's categorized as such. The accounting rate of return considers the profitability of a project based on the accounting amounts found in the company's statements. Net income amounts are not adjusted for the time value of money, which is why it's considered a non-discounted model.

In these models, $1,000 earned in the fourth year is just as valuable as $1,000 earned today. The calculation is straightforward. The projected revenue earned is divided by the amount of money that needs to be invested, and the return is calculated. If a company needs to invest $100,000 and can earn $10,000 in year one, $9,000 in year two, and $15,000 in year three, the individual returns are as follows:

- year one = 10,000/100,000 = 10%

- year two = 9,000/100,000 = 9%
- year three = 15,000/100,000 = 15%

These rates of return are compared to the alternatives and the best one is chosen. Some companies even calculate the average of the yearly returns and choose the one with the highest average. The advantage of this method is that it's easy to compute returns. You can perform these calculations on the back of an envelope and don't need special calculators or spreadsheets.

The downside is that if your company is large and has multiple projects it could potentially invest in, and if these projects stretch to more than a decade, this is a very rudimentary method of computing rates of return.

Payback

The payback method uses cash flows generated from the project instead of net income. This is also a non-discounted model like the previous method. Let's stick with the previous example to see how it works. Let's assume for simplicity's sake that the net income assumed in the previous section is equal to the cash flow. Let's map these out according to the table below. Remember that the investment is $100,000:

Year	Cash Flow
1	10,000
2	9,000
3	15,000
4	20,000
5	20,000
6	20,000
7	20,000

The payback method determines how long it will take for the company to earn its investment back. Based on these cash flows we can see that it will take a little under seven years to recover the investment. This is a long time for a company to wait. You might argue that the rate of return is high as we saw in the previous method. However, the payback method assumes that the invested amount cannot be recovered by any means.

For example, if the asset that is being created cannot be sold for even pennies on the dollar, companies need to first recover their costs before earning a profit. The previous method assumes that the asset being created has some salvage value and therefore ignores the need to recover investment costs before computing returns.

NPV

NPV stands for net present value, as you've learned. This is a discounted cash flow model. Every NPV calculation has a hurdle rate, or a risk-free rate. This is the rate that money would grow at, assuming everything stayed the same. For example, a profitable business might have a primary line of business that grows at 12% per year. If this is the case, here's what the time of value of a dollar earned looks like:

Today	1
In 1 year's time	0.89
In 2 years time	0.8
In 3 years time	0.71
In 4 years time	0.64
In 5 years time	0.57
In 6 years time	0.51
In 7 years time	0.45
In 8 years time	0.4
In 9 years time	0.36
In 10 years time	0.32

Here's how you would interpret this table. If you received one dollar 10 years from today, it would be the same as receiving 32 cents today. Let's look at a sample NPV calculation to see how it works. I'll assume a 12% risk-free rate once again.

Time	Cash flow before discounting	Discount factor	Present value
Today	-100,000	1	-100,000
1	21,000	0.89	18,690
2	24,000	0.8	19,200
3	22,000	0.71	15,620
4	23,000	0.64	14,720
5	25,000	0.57	14,250
6	23,000	0.51	11,730
7	20,000	0.45	9,000

The final step is to sum all the values in the final column. In this case, the sum is $3,210. A positive value indicates that this project is earning a greater rate of return than 12% and should therefore be invested in. If the sum is zero or is negative, then the company is better off sticking to its current investment options.

Internal Rate of Return

The IRR method is the same as the NPV method except it focuses on the rate of return the project produces. The way this is done is by playing around with the hurdle rate that would produce an NPV of zero. From our previous example, we would increase the hurdle rate until it resulted in an NPV of zero for this project. In this example, this would be close to 16%. This is the IRR of the project.

Every proposed investment's IRR is compared to one another and the one with the highest IRR is chosen.

The NPV and IRR model is used to evaluate what another company is worth. Let's say company A is growing its earnings at 10% every year and is considering buying out one of its competitors for $1 million. It has two choices. It could reinvest the million dollars into its own business and earn 10% through earnings growth, or it could invest it into the second company and see what it can earn.

The decision to buy the other company hinges on the NPV of the cash flows the second company will bring to company A. If the NPV of those cash flows is positive after taking the 10% hurdle rate into account, buying it makes sense for company A. If not, they're better off reinvesting it into their own business.

Strictly speaking, NPV and IRR aren't accounting functions in the sense that they affect financial statement preparation.

However, they are used extensively in valuation and as a business owner, it's imperative that you understand how the time value of money works. Many business owners are unaware of the concept of the time value of money, which is why I spent some time discussing how it affects business decisions.

The way your accounting statements are prepared affects the value of your business. The discounted cash flow models bring all the elements of your accounting statements together and reduces them to a single value that indicates what your business is worth.

Conclusion

Accounting is a far deeper subject than what you've read in this book. However, all of the chapters in this book cover the most important topics that you ought to be aware of. Remember that your objective isn't to become an expert at all of them. Instead, you need to understand the basics of each aspect of accounting, and this is what I've presented in this book. The next time your accountant starts talking about these subjects, you'll be able to follow along and ask intelligent questions, instead of simply accepting whatever they say.

Everything begins with your bookkeeping, and the double-entry accounting system underpins everything to do with the way your business' numbers are accounted for. All of the major financial statements have their origin in the GL. If you can understand how GL entries are recorded and how it works, you'll have no issues figuring out how the income statement, balance sheet, and the cash flow statement are prepared.

The balance sheet contains all the information about your business' assets and liabilities. It also lists the shareholders' equity, which is the measure of how much of your company you own. Many companies have large balance sheets thanks to debt. Measuring the return earned on equity is informative and gives a clear picture of how leveraged a business is.

There are a few important ratios connected to the balance sheet that you've learned about. Remember that they're only as good as the numbers behind them. The income statement is another important financial statement and it's all about profit and loss. Accounting for COGS is essential when determining your bottom-line net income, along with clearly differentiating between operating and capital expenditures.

The last accounting statement that is essential is the SCF. This lists the free cash flows your business produces and helps close the gap between the accrual accounting produced net income and actual cash flow into your bank accounts. If you're considering buying another company, pay attention to their free cash flow and compare it to the net income for anomalies.

All of the numbers in these statements can be put together to arrive at a number that signifies what a business is worth. Plugging net income or free cash flow into a discounted cash flow model like the NPV is a great way of figuring out how much a business is truly worth and whether it's worth investing in. Discounted models can be complicated and for this reason, you can use simpler models. However, the time value of money is a real thing and has to always be accounted for. If the project is simple and doesn't have lengthy cash flow periods, then a non-discounted model is appropriate.

I'm positive you've gained massive insights into how accounting statements for businesses are prepared after reading this. I hope you've enjoyed this book, and now feel more confident when approaching the topic of accounting in your business!

www.ingramcontent.com/pod-product-compliance
Lightning Source LLC
LaVergne TN
LVHW011738060526
838200LV00051B/3234